Incredibly Easy
Recipes

Publications International, Ltd.
Favorite Brand Name Recipes at www.fbnr.com

ISBN-13: 978-1-4127-7787-2
ISBN-10: 1-4127-7787-9

Library of Congress Control Number: 2008940480

Pictured on the front cover: VELVEETA Double-Decker Nachos *(page 112)*.

Pictured on the back cover: VELVEETA Tex-Mex Beef and Potatoes *(page 80)*.

Microwave Cooking: Microwave ovens vary in wattage. Use the cooking times as guidelines and check for doneness before adding more time.

Preparation/Cooking Times: Preparation times are based on the approximate amount of time required to assemble the recipe before cooking, baking, chilling, or serving. These times include preparation steps such as measuring, chopping, and mixing. The fact that some preparations and cooking can be done simultaneously is taken into account. Preparation of optional ingredients and serving suggestions is not included.

contents

4

36

120

116

party-time
dips

VELVEETA ultimate queso dip

PREP: 5 min. | TOTAL: 10 min. | MAKES: 3 cups or 24 servings, 2 Tbsp. each.

▶ what you need!

 **+**

1 lb. (16 oz.)
VELVEETA Pasteurized
Prepared Cheese
Product, cut into
½-inch cubes

1 can (10 oz.)
RO*TEL Diced
Tomatoes &
Green Chilies,
undrained

▶ make it!

1. **MIX** ingredients in microwaveable bowl.

2. **MICROWAVE** on HIGH 5 min. or until VELVEETA is completely melted, stirring after 3 min.

3. **SERVE** with assorted cut-up fresh vegetables, WHEAT THINS Crackers or tortilla chips.

SIZE-WISE:
When eating appetizers at a social occasion, preview your choices and decide which you'd like to try instead of taking some of each.

*Ro*Tel is a product of ConAgra Foods, Inc.*

cheesy pizza dip

PREP: 10 min. | TOTAL: 15 min. | MAKES: 2½ cups or 20 servings, 2 Tbsp. each.

▶ what you need!

1 lb. (16 oz.) VELVEETA Pasteurized Prepared Cheese Product, cut into ½-inch cubes

1 tomato, chopped

20 pepperoni slices (1½ oz.), chopped

▶ make it!

1. **COMBINE** ingredients in 1½-qt. microwaveable bowl.

2. **MICROWAVE** on HIGH 4 to 5 min. or until VELVEETA is completely melted, stirring every 2 min.

3. **SERVE** hot with breadsticks or assorted cut-up fresh vegetables.

CREATIVE LEFTOVERS:
Refrigerate any leftover dip. Reheat and drizzle over hot baked potatoes or cooked pasta for an easy cheesy sauce.

cheesy spinach and bacon dip

PREP: 10 min. | TOTAL: 15 min. | MAKES: 4 cups or 32 servings, 2 Tbsp. each.

▶ what you need!

1 pkg. (10 oz.) frozen chopped spinach, thawed, drained

1 lb. (16 oz.) VELVEETA Pasteurized Prepared Cheese Product, cut into ½-inch cubes

4 oz. (½ of 8-oz. pkg.) PHILADELPHIA Cream Cheese, cubed

1 can (10 oz.) RO*TEL Diced Tomatoes & Green Chilies, undrained

8 slices OSCAR MAYER Bacon, cooked, crumbled

▶ make it!

1. **MICROWAVE** all ingredients in microwaveable bowl on HIGH 5 min. or until VELVEETA is completely melted and mixture is well blended, stirring after 3 min.

2. **SERVE** with tortilla chips and cut-up fresh vegetables.

USE YOUR SLOW COOKER:
When serving this dip at a party, pour the prepared dip into a small slow cooker set on LOW. This will keep the dip warm and at the ideal consistency for several hours. For best results, stir the dip occasionally to prevent hot spots.

*Ro*Tel is a product of ConAgra Foods, Inc.*

hot broccoli dip

PREP: 30 min. | TOTAL: 30 min. | MAKES: 2½ cups or 20 servings, 2 Tbsp. each.

▶ what you need!

1 loaf (1½ lb.) round sourdough bread

½ cup chopped celery

½ cup chopped red peppers

¼ cup chopped onions

2 Tbsp. butter or margarine

1 lb. (16 oz.) VELVEETA Pasteurized Prepared Cheese Product, cut into ½-inch cubes

1 pkg. (10 oz.) frozen chopped broccoli, thawed, drained

¼ tsp. dried rosemary leaves, crushed

Few drops hot pepper sauce

▶ make it!

1. **HEAT** oven to 350°F. Cut slice from top of bread loaf; remove center, leaving 1-inch-thick shell. Cut removed bread into bite-size pieces. Cover shell with top of bread; place on baking sheet with bread pieces. Bake 15 min. Cool slightly.

2. **MEANWHILE**, cook and stir celery, red peppers and onions in butter in medium saucepan on medium heat until tender. Add VELVEETA; cook on low heat until melted, stirring frequently. Add broccoli, rosemary and hot pepper sauce; cook until heated through, stirring constantly.

3. **SPOON** into bread loaf. Serve with toasted bread pieces, NABISCO Crackers and/or assorted cut-up fresh vegetables.

USE YOUR MICROWAVE:
Microwave celery, red peppers, onions and butter in 2-qt. microwaveable bowl on HIGH 1 min. Add VELVEETA, broccoli, rosemary and hot pepper sauce; mix well. Microwave 5 to 6 min. or until VELVEETA is melted, stirring after 3 min.

VELVEETA bacon and green onion dip

PREP: 5 min. | TOTAL: 10 min. | MAKES: 2½ cups or 20 servings, 2 Tbsp. each.

▶ what you need!

1 lb. (16 oz.) VELVEETA Pasteurized Prepared Cheese Product, cut into ½-inch cubes

4 green onions, sliced

½ cup OSCAR MAYER Bacon Pieces

½ cup BREAKSTONE'S or KNUDSEN Sour Cream

▶ make it!

1. **MIX** VELVEETA, onions and bacon in large microwaveable bowl. Microwave on HIGH 5 min. or until VELVEETA is completely melted, stirring after 3 min.

2. **STIR** in sour cream.

3. **SERVE** with assorted cut-up fresh vegetables or WHEAT THINS Crackers.

TO HALVE:
Cut ingredients in half. Mix ingredients in 1-qt. microwaveable bowl. Microwave on HIGH 3 to 4 min. or until VELVEETA is completely melted, stirring after 2 min. Serve as directed. Makes 10 servings, 2 Tbsp. each.

VELVEETA cheesy bean dip

PREP: 5 min. | TOTAL: 11 min. | MAKES: 3¼ cups or 26 servings, 2 Tbsp. each.

▶ what you need!

1 lb. (16 oz.) VELVEETA Mexican Pasteurized Prepared Cheese Product, cut into ½-inch cubes

1 can (16 oz.) TACO BELL® HOME ORIGINALS® Refried Beans

½ cup TACO BELL® HOME ORIGINALS® Thick 'N Chunky Salsa

▶ make it!

1. **MIX** all ingredients in microwaveable bowl.

2. **MICROWAVE** on HIGH 5 to 6 min. or until VELVEETA is completely melted and mixture is well blended, stirring after 3 min.

3. **SERVE** with assorted cut-up fresh vegetables or tortilla chips.

SPECIAL EXTRA:
To serve in a bread bowl, cut a lengthwise slice from the top of 1-lb. round bread loaf. Remove center of loaf, leaving 1-inch-thick shell. Cut top of loaf and removed bread into bite-size pieces to serve with dip. Fill bread bowl with hot dip just before serving.

TACO BELL® and HOME ORIGINALS® are trademarks owned and licensed by Taco Bell Corp.

VELVEETA chili dip

PREP: 5 min. | TOTAL: 10 min. | MAKES: 3 cups or 24 servings, 2 Tbsp. each.

▶ what you need!

1 lb. (16 oz.) VELVEETA Pasteurized Prepared Cheese Product, cut into ½-inch cubes

1 can (15 oz.) chili (with or without beans)

▶ make it!

1. MIX VELVEETA and chili in microwaveable bowl.

2. MICROWAVE on HIGH 5 min. or until VELVEETA is completely melted and mixture is well blended, stirring after 3 min.

3. SERVE with tortilla chips, RITZ Toasted Chips or assorted cut-up fresh vegetables.

TO SERVE A CROWD:
Mix 1½ lb. (24 oz.) VELVEETA Pasteurized Prepared Cheese Product, cut up, and 2 cups canned chili in 2½-quart microwaveable bowl on HIGH 4 min.; stir. Microwave 4 to 6 min. or until VELVEETA is melted, stirring every 2 min.; stir. Serve as directed. Makes 5 cups or 40 servings, 2 Tbsp. each.

VELVEETA chipotle dip

PREP: 10 min. | TOTAL: 16 min. | MAKES: 3¼ cups or 26 servings, 2 Tbsp. each.

▶ what you need!

1 lb. (16 oz.) VELVEETA Pasteurized Prepared Cheese Product, cut into
½-inch cubes

2 Tbsp. chipotle peppers in adobo sauce, chopped

1 container (16 oz.) BREAKSTONE'S or KNUDSEN Sour Cream

▶ make it!

1. **MIX** VELVEETA and peppers in microwaveable bowl.

2. **MICROWAVE** on HIGH 4 to 6 min. or until VELVEETA is completely melted, stirring after 3 min. Stir in sour cream.

3. **SERVE** with assorted cut-up fresh vegetables.

TO HALVE:
Prepare as directed, cutting all ingredients in half. Makes about 1½ cups or 13 servings, about 2 Tbsp. each.

VELVEETA hot 'n cheesy crab dip

PREP: 5 min. | TOTAL: 10 min. | MAKES: 2½ cups or 20 servings, 2 Tbsp. each.

▶ what you need!

1 lb. (16 oz.) VELVEETA Pasteurized Prepared Cheese Product, cut into ½-inch cubes

1 can (6½ oz.) crabmeat, drained, flaked

4 green onions, sliced

½ cup chopped red peppers

½ cup BREAKSTONE'S or KNUDSEN Sour Cream

⅛ tsp. ground red pepper (cayenne)

▶ make it!

1. **MIX** first 4 ingredients in large microwaveable bowl. Microwave on HIGH 5 min. or until VELVEETA is completely melted, stirring after 3 min.

2. **STIR** in remaining ingredients.

3. **SERVE** with WHEAT THINS Crackers or assorted cut-up fresh vegetables.

KEEPING IT SAFE:
Hot dips should be discarded after setting at room temperature for 2 hours or longer.

VELVEETA mexican dip

PREP: 5 min. | TOTAL: 7 min. 30 sec. | MAKES: 1¼ cups or 10 servings, 2 Tbsp. each.

▶ what you need!

 **+**

½ lb. (8 oz.) VELVEETA
Mexican Pasteurized
Prepared Cheese
Product, cut into
½-inch cubes

½ cup
BREAKSTONE'S
or KNUDSEN
Sour Cream

▶ make it!

1. **MICROWAVE** VELVEETA in 1½-qt. microwaveable bowl on HIGH 2 min.; stir until completely melted.

2. **STIR** in sour cream. Microwave 30 sec.; stir.

3. **SERVE** with assorted cut-up fresh vegetables, WHEAT THINS Crackers or baked tortilla chips.

SPECIAL EXTRA:
For an easy cheesy sauce, serve over hot baked potatoes or cooked pasta.

VELVEETA ranch dip

PREP: 5 min. | TOTAL: 10 min. | MAKES: 3¼ cups or 26 servings, 2 Tbsp. each.

▸ what you need!

 **+**  **+**

| 1 lb. (16 oz.) VELVEETA Pasteurized Prepared Cheese Product, cut into ½-inch cubes | 1 container (8 oz.) BREAKSTONE'S or KNUDSEN Sour Cream | 1 cup KRAFT Ranch Dressing |

▸ make it!

1. **MIX** all ingredients in microwaveable bowl.

2. **MICROWAVE** on HIGH 6 min. or until VELVEETA is completely melted and mixture is well blended, stirring every 2 min.

3. **SERVE** with assorted cut-up fresh vegetables or your favorite NABISCO Crackers.

VELVEETA ZESTY RANCH DIP:
Add 1 undrained can (10 oz.) RO*TEL Diced Tomatoes and Green Chilies to dip ingredients before microwaving. Increase the microwave time to 8 min., stirring after every 2 min. Serve as directed.

*Ro*Tel is a product of ConAgra Foods, Inc.*

VELVEETA salsa dip

PREP: 5 min. | TOTAL: 10 min. | MAKES: 2½ cups or 20 servings, 2 Tbsp. each.

▶ what you need!

1 lb. (16 oz.) VELVEETA Pasteurized Prepared Cheese Product, cut into ½-inch cubes

1 cup TACO BELL® HOME ORIGINALS® Thick 'N Chunky Salsa

▶ make it!

1. **MIX** ingredients in microwaveable bowl.

2. **MICROWAVE** on HIGH 5 min. or until VELVEETA is completely melted, stirring after 3 min.

3. **SERVE** with tortilla chips, assorted cut-up fresh vegetables or RITZ Toasted Chips Original.

HOW TO HALVE:
Prepare cutting ingredients in half and reducing the microwave time to 3 to 4 min. or until VELVEETA is completely melted, stirring after 2 min. Makes 1½ cups or 12 servings, 2 Tbsp. each.

TACO BELL® and HOME ORIGINALS® are trademarks owned and licensed by Taco Bell Corp.

VELVEETA southwestern chicken dip

PREP: 10 min. | TOTAL: 17 min. | MAKES: 3½ cups or 28 servings, 2 Tbsp. each.

▶ what you need!

- 1 lb. (16 oz.) VELVEETA Pasteurized Prepared Cheese Product, cut into ½-inch cubes
- 1 can (10 oz.) RO*TEL Diced Tomatoes & Green Chilies, drained
- 1 pkg. (6 oz.) OSCAR MAYER Southwestern Seasoned or Grilled Chicken Breast Strips, chopped
- 2 green onions, chopped

▶ make it!

1. **MIX** all ingredients in microwaveable bowl.

2. **MICROWAVE** on HIGH 6 to 7 min. or until VELVEETA is completely melted and mixture is well blended, stirring every 3 min.

3. **SERVE** with tortilla chips or assorted cut-up fresh vegetables.

SUBSTITUTE:
Substitute ½ lb. ground beef, cooked and drained, for the chopped chicken breast strips.

*Ro*Tel is a product of ConAgra Foods, Inc.*

VELVEETA southwestern corn dip

PREP: 5 min. | TOTAL: 10 min. | MAKES: 3½ cups or 28 servings, 2 Tbsp. each.

▶ what you need!

1 lb. (16 oz.) VELVEETA Pasteurized Prepared Cheese Product, cut into ½-inch cubes

1 can (11 oz.) corn with red and green peppers, drained

3 jalapeño peppers, seeded, minced

1 red onion, finely chopped

½ cup fresh cilantro, finely chopped

½ cup BREAKSTONE'S or KNUDSEN Sour Cream

▶ make it!

1. **MIX** VELVEETA and corn in large microwaveable bowl.

2. **MICROWAVE** on HIGH 5 min. or until VELVEETA is completely melted, stirring after 3 min. Stir in remaining ingredients.

3. **SERVE** with WHEAT THINS Crackers or assorted cut-up fresh vegetables.

HOW TO MAKE IT SPICY:
Save the seeds from 1 of the jalapeños and add to the dip. Or if you like it really fiery, no need to seed the peppers at all—simply slice off the stems and chop.

VELVEETA spicy buffalo dip

PREP: 5 min. | TOTAL: 10 min. | MAKES: 2¾ cups or 22 servings, 2 Tbsp. each.

► what you need!

1 lb. (16 oz.) VELVEETA Pasteurized Prepared Cheese Product, cut into ½-inch cubes

1 cup BREAKSTONE'S or KNUDSEN Sour Cream

¼ cup cayenne pepper sauce for Buffalo wings

¼ cup KRAFT Natural Blue Cheese Crumbles

2 green onions, sliced

► make it!

1. **MIX** VELVEETA, sour cream and pepper sauce in large microwaveable bowl.

2. **MICROWAVE** on HIGH 5 min. or until VELVEETA is completely melted, stirring after 3 min. Stir in remaining ingredients.

3. **SERVE** with celery and carrot sticks.

VARIATION:
Prepare using VELVEETA 2% Milk Pasteurized Prepared Cheese Product.

VELVEETA spicy cheeseburger dip

PREP: 5 min. | TOTAL: 10 min. | MAKES: 4½ cups or 36 servings, 2 Tbsp. each.

▶ what you need!

1 lb. (16 oz.) VELVEETA Pasteurized Prepared Cheese Product, cut into ½-inch cubes

1 can (10 oz.) RO*TEL Diced Tomatoes & Green Chilies, undrained

1 cup KRAFT Shredded Low-Moisture Part-Skim Mozzarella Cheese

½ lb. ground beef, cooked, drained

4 green onions, sliced

▶ make it!

1. **MIX** all ingredients except onions in microwaveable bowl.

2. **MICROWAVE** on HIGH 5 min. or until VELVEETA is melted, stirring after 3 min. Stir in onions.

3. **SERVE** with RITZ Crackers and assorted cut-up fresh vegetables.

USE YOUR STOVE:
Mix all ingredients except onions in medium saucepan; cook on medium heat 5 to 7 min. or until VELVEETA is melted, stirring frequently. Stir in onions. Serve as directed.

*Ro*Tel is a product of ConAgra Foods, Inc.*

VELVEETA spicy sausage dip

PREP: 5 min. | TOTAL: 10 min. | MAKES: 1 qt. or 32 servings, 2 Tbsp. each.

▶ what you need!

1 lb. (16 oz.) VELVEETA Pasteurized Prepared Cheese Product, cut into ½-inch cubes

½ lb. pork sausage, cooked, drained

1 can (10 oz.) RO*TEL Diced Tomatoes & Green Chilies, undrained

▶ make it!

1. **MIX** all ingredients in microwaveable bowl.

2. **MICROWAVE** on HIGH 5 min. or until VELVEETA is completely melted, stirring after 3 min.

3. **SERVE** with tortilla chips or WHEAT THINS Crackers.

STORAGE KNOW-HOW:
Store leftover dip in airtight container in refrigerator up to 3 days. Reheat dip in microwave before serving.

*Ro*Tel is a product of ConAgra Foods, Inc.*

crowd-pleasing entrées

VELVEETA ultimate macaroni & cheese

PREP: 5 min. | TOTAL: 20 min. | MAKES: 4 servings, 1 cup each.

▶ what you need!

2 cups elbow macaroni, uncooked

¾ lb. (12 oz.) VELVEETA Pasteurized Prepared Cheese Product, cut into ½-inch cubes

⅓ cup milk

⅛ tsp. black pepper

▶ make it!

1. **COOK** macaroni in large saucepan as directed on package; drain well. Return to pan.

2. **STIR** in remaining ingredients; cook on low heat until VELVEETA is completely melted and mixture is well blended, stirring frequently.

VARIATION:
Prepare as directed; spoon into 2-qt. casserole. Bake at 350°F for 25 min.

beef enchiladas olé

PREP: 20 min. | MICROWAVE: 6 min. | MAKES: 6 servings.

▶ what you need!

1 lb. ground beef

½ lb. (8 oz.) VELVEETA Mexican Pasteurized Prepared Cheese Product, cut into ½-inch cubes, divided

1 cup TACO BELL® HOME ORIGINALS® Thick 'N Chunky Salsa, divided

12 flour tortillas

▶ make it!

1. **BROWN** meat in large skillet; drain. Stir in half each of the Mexican VELVEETA and salsa; cook until VELVEETA is completely melted, stirring frequently.

2. **SPOON** scant ¼ cup meat mixture down center of each tortilla; roll up. Place, seam-sides down, in single layer in microwaveable dish. Top with remaining salsa and VELVEETA; cover with waxed paper.

3. **MICROWAVE** on HIGH 4 to 6 min. or until VELVEETA is melted.

SUBSTITUTE:
Try leaner cuts of ground beef, such as ground round or ground sirloin, in place of ground beef.

TACO BELL® and HOME ORIGINALS® are trademarks owned and licensed by Taco Bell Corp.

VELVEETA cheeseburger mac

PREP: 5 min. | TOTAL: 35 min. | MAKES: 6 servings.

▶ what you need!

1 lb. ground beef

2¾ cups water

⅓ cup ketchup

1 tsp. onion powder

2 cups elbow macaroni, uncooked

½ lb. (8 oz.) VELVEETA Pasteurized Prepared Cheese Product, cut into ½-inch cubes

▶ make it!

1. **BROWN** meat in large skillet; drain.

2. **ADD** water, ketchup and onion powder; mix well. Bring to boil. Stir in macaroni; cover. Simmer on medium-low heat 8 to 10 min. or until macaroni is tender.

3. **STIR** in VELVEETA; cook until melted, stirring occasionally.

SERVING SUGGESTION:
Serve with a cooked crisp green vegetable, such as broccoli.

cheesy chicken & broccoli bake

PREP: **10 min.** | TOTAL: **50 min.** | MAKES: 6 servings, about 1⅓ cups each.

▶ what you need!

1 pkg. (6 oz.) STOVE TOP Stuffing Mix for Chicken

1½ lb. boneless skinless chicken breasts, cut into bite-size pieces

1 pkg. (16 oz.) frozen broccoli florets, thawed, drained

1 can (10¾ oz.) reduced-sodium condensed cream of chicken soup

½ lb. (8 oz.) VELVEETA Pasteurized Prepared Cheese Product, cut into ½-inch cubes

▶ make it!

1.

HEAT oven to 400°F. Prepare stuffing mix as directed on package; set aside.

2.

COMBINE remaining ingredients; spoon into 13×9-inch baking dish. Top with stuffing.

3.

BAKE 40 min. or until chicken is done.

SUBSTITUTE:
Substitute frozen mixed vegetables, thawed and drained, for the broccoli florets.

cheesy italian pasta bake

PREP: 25 min. | TOTAL: 45 min. | MAKES: 6 servings, 1½ cups each.

▶ what you need!

1½ cups whole wheat wagon wheel pasta, uncooked

1 lb. extra lean ground beef

1 large carrot, shredded

1 large zucchini, shredded

1 red pepper, chopped

1 can (8 oz.) pizza sauce

½ lb. (8 oz.) VELVEETA 2% Milk Pasteurized Prepared Cheese Product, cut into ½-inch cubes

½ cup KRAFT Grated Parmesan Cheese

▶ make it!

1. **HEAT** oven to 350°F. Cook pasta as directed on package. Meanwhile, brown meat in large nonstick skillet on medium-high heat. Stir in vegetables and sauce; cook 5 min. or until vegetables are tender. Drain pasta. Add to meat mixture along with VELVEETA; mix well.

2. **SPOON** into 8-inch square baking dish sprayed with cooking spray; sprinkle with Parmesan.

3. **BAKE** 15 to 20 min. or until heated through.

SUBSTITUTE:
Prepare using any other bite-size shaped pasta.

cheesy red beans & rice

PREP: 10 min. | TOTAL: 1 hour | MAKES: 6 servings, 1 cup each.

▶ what you need!

1 can (15½ oz.) kidney beans, drained, rinsed

1 can (10 oz.) RO*TEL Diced Tomatoes & Green Chilies, undrained

2 cups instant white rice, uncooked

2 cups water

7 oz. (½ of 14-oz. pkg.) OSCAR MAYER Turkey Smoked Sausage, sliced, halved

6 oz. VELVEETA Pasteurized Prepared Cheese Product, cut into ½-inch cubes

1 small onion, chopped

2 tsp. chili powder

▶ make it!

1. **HEAT** oven to 350°F. Combine all ingredients.

2. **SPOON** into 13×9-inch baking dish sprayed with cooking spray.

3. **BAKE** 45 to 50 min. or until rice is tender and mixture is heated through.

SUBSTITUTE:
Prepare using VELVEETA 2% Milk Pasteurized Prepared Cheese Product.

*Ro*Tel is a product of ConAgra Foods, Inc*

chicken enchiladas

PREP: 20 min. | TOTAL: 40 min. | MAKES: 4 servings.

▶ what you need!

2 cups chopped cooked chicken or turkey

1 green pepper, chopped

4 oz. (½ of 8-oz. pkg.) PHILADELPHIA Cream Cheese, cubed

½ cup TACO BELL® HOME ORIGINALS® Thick 'N Chunky Salsa, divided

8 TACO BELL® HOME ORIGINALS® Flour Tortillas

¼ lb. (4 oz.) VELVEETA Pasteurized Prepared Cheese Product, cut into
   ½-inch cubes

1 Tbsp. milk

▶ make it!

1. **HEAT** oven to 350°F. Mix chicken, peppers, cream cheese and ¼ cup salsa in saucepan; cook on low heat until cream cheese is melted, stirring occasionally.

2. **SPOON** ⅓ cup chicken mixture down center of each tortilla; roll up. Place, seam-sides down, in lightly greased 13×9-inch baking dish; set aside. Cook VELVEETA and milk in saucepan on low heat until VELVEETA is completely melted, stirring frequently. Pour over enchiladas; cover with foil.

3. **BAKE** 20 min. or until heated through. Top with remaining salsa.

SHORTCUT:
Substitute 1 pkg. (6 oz.) OSCAR MAYER Deli Fresh Oven Roasted Chicken Breast Cuts for the chopped cooked fresh chicken.

TACO BELL® and HOME ORIGINALS® are trademarks owned and licensed by Taco Bell Corp.

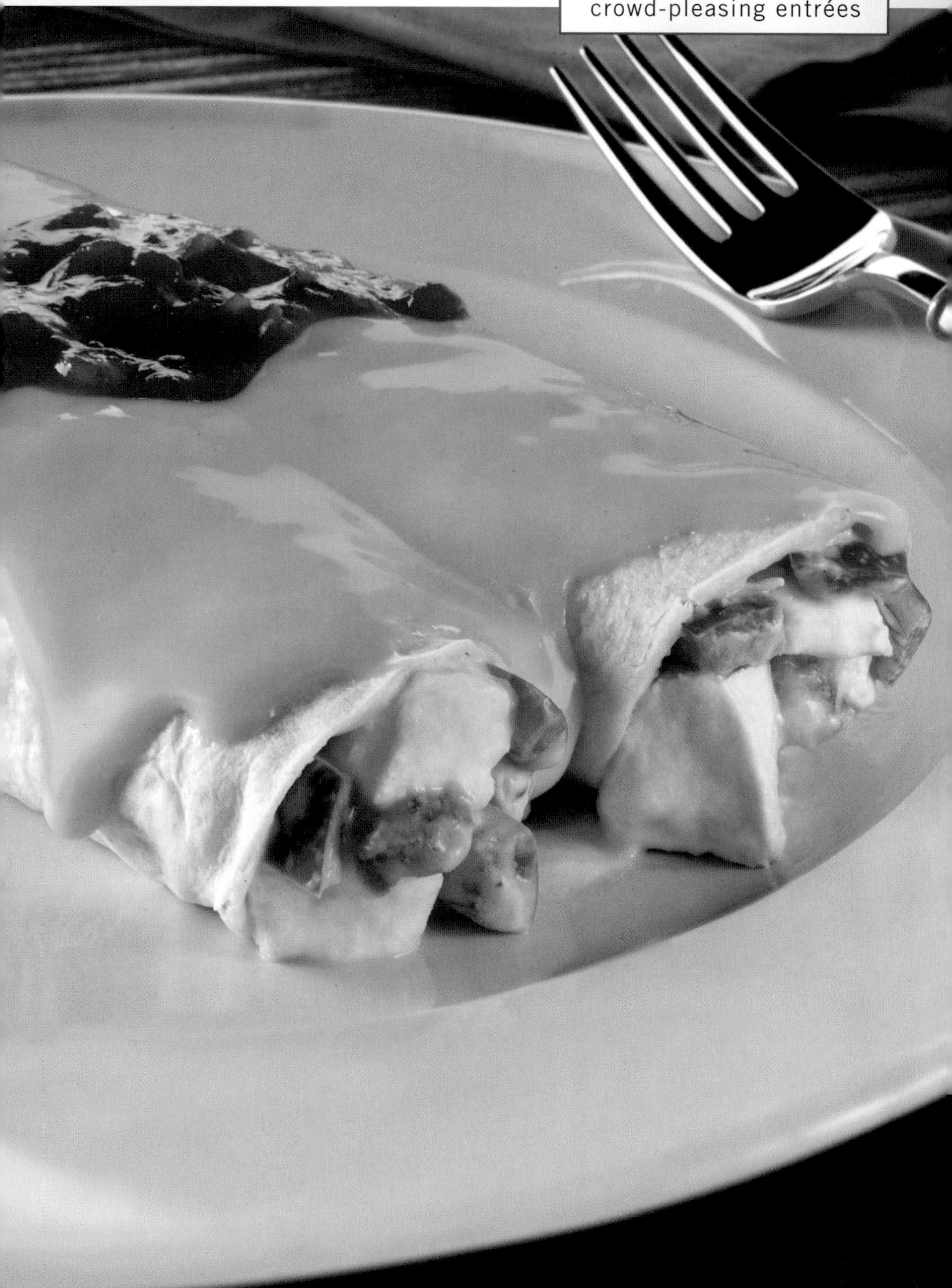

chicken fiesta chili mac

PREP: 15 min. | TOTAL: 35 min. | MAKES: 6 servings.

▶ what you need!

1½ cups elbow macaroni, uncooked

1 lb. boneless skinless chicken breasts, cut into strips

1 can (15 oz.) chili with beans

½ lb. (8 oz.) VELVEETA Pasteurized Prepared Cheese Product, cut into ½-inch cubes

½ cup TACO BELL® HOME ORIGINALS® Thick 'N Chunky Salsa

½ cup chopped green peppers

2 cloves garlic, minced

▶ make it!

1. **HEAT** oven to 350°F. Cook macaroni as directed on package. Meanwhile, cook chicken in large nonstick skillet sprayed with cooking spray 5 to 7 min. or until done, stirring frequently.

2. **DRAIN** macaroni. Add to chicken in skillet along with remaining ingredients; mix well. Spoon into 13×9-inch baking dish sprayed with cooking spray.

3. **BAKE** 20 min. or until heated through. Stir before serving.

SERVING SUGGESTION:
Serve this family-pleasing main dish with a crisp mixed green salad tossed with your favorite KRAFT Dressing.

TACO BELL® and HOME ORIGINALS® are trademarks owned and licensed by Taco Bell Corp.

creamy mexican chicken pasta

PREP: **10** min. | TOTAL: **25** min. | MAKES: **6** servings.

▶ what you need!

3 cups farfalle (bow-tie pasta), uncooked

1¼ lb. boneless skinless chicken breasts, cut into strips

½ lb. (8 oz.) VELVEETA Pasteurized Prepared Cheese Product, cut into ½-inch cubes

1 can (10¾ oz.) condensed cream of mushroom soup

1 cup TACO BELL® HOME ORIGINALS® Thick 'N Chunky Salsa

¼ cup milk

▶ make it!

1. **COOK** pasta in large saucepan as directed on package. Meanwhile, cook chicken in skillet sprayed with cooking spray on medium heat 4 to 5 min. or until done, stirring occasionally.

2. **DRAIN** pasta; return to saucepan. Stir in chicken and all remaining ingredients. Cook on low heat until VELVEETA is completely melted and mixture is well blended, stirring occasionally.

HOW TO CUBE VELVEETA:
Cut measured amount of VELVEETA into ½-inch-thick slices. Then, cut each slice crosswise in both directions to make cubes.

TACO BELL® and HOME ORIGINALS® are trademarks owned and licensed by Taco Bell Corp.

fish & vegetable platter with cheesy garlic-cilantro sauce

PREP: 15 min. | TOTAL: 15 min. | MAKES: 6 servings.

▶ what you need!

½ lb. (8 oz.) VELVEETA Pasteurized Prepared Cheese Product, cut into ½-inch cubes

¼ cup milk

1 clove garlic, minced

1 Tbsp. chopped fresh cilantro

1½ lb. cod fillets or steaks, cooked

4 cups cut-up mixed fresh vegetables (broccoli, carrots, peppers, squash), cooked

▶ make it!

1. **COMBINE** VELVEETA, milk and garlic in saucepan.

2. **COOK** on low heat until VELVEETA is completely melted and mixture is well blended, stirring frequently. Stir in cilantro.

3. **SPOON** over fish and vegetables.

SPECIAL EXTRA:
Add 1 chopped fresh jalapeño pepper to the sauce along with the cilantro.

gram's chicken pot pie updated

PREP 10 min. | TOTAL: 40 min. | MAKES: 6 servings.

▶ what you need!

1 lb. boneless skinless chicken breasts, cut into bite-size pieces

2 Tbsp. KRAFT Light Zesty Italian Dressing

2 cups frozen mixed vegetables

1 can (10¾ oz.) reduced sodium condensed cream of chicken soup

¼ lb. (4 oz.) VELVEETA 2% Milk Pasteurized Prepared Cheese Product, cut into ½-inch cubes

1 sheet frozen puff pastry (½ of 17.3-oz. pkg.), thawed

1 egg, beaten

▶ make it!

1. **HEAT** oven to 400°F. Cook and stir chicken in dressing in large skillet on medium heat 5 min. or until done. Stir in vegetables, soup and VELVEETA. Spoon into greased 9-inch square baking dish.

2. **UNFOLD** pastry sheet; place over chicken mixture. Fold under edges of pastry; press onto top of baking dish to seal. Brush with egg. Cut several slits in crust to permit steam to escape. Place on baking sheet.

3. **BAKE** 30 min. or until crust is deep golden brown. Let stand 5 min.

HOW TO THAW PASTRY SHEETS:
Remove pastry sheet from freezer; cover with plastic wrap. Thaw at room temperature for 30 min. or in refrigerator for 4 hours. Thawed wrapped pastry sheets can be stored in refrigerator up to 2 days before using as desired.

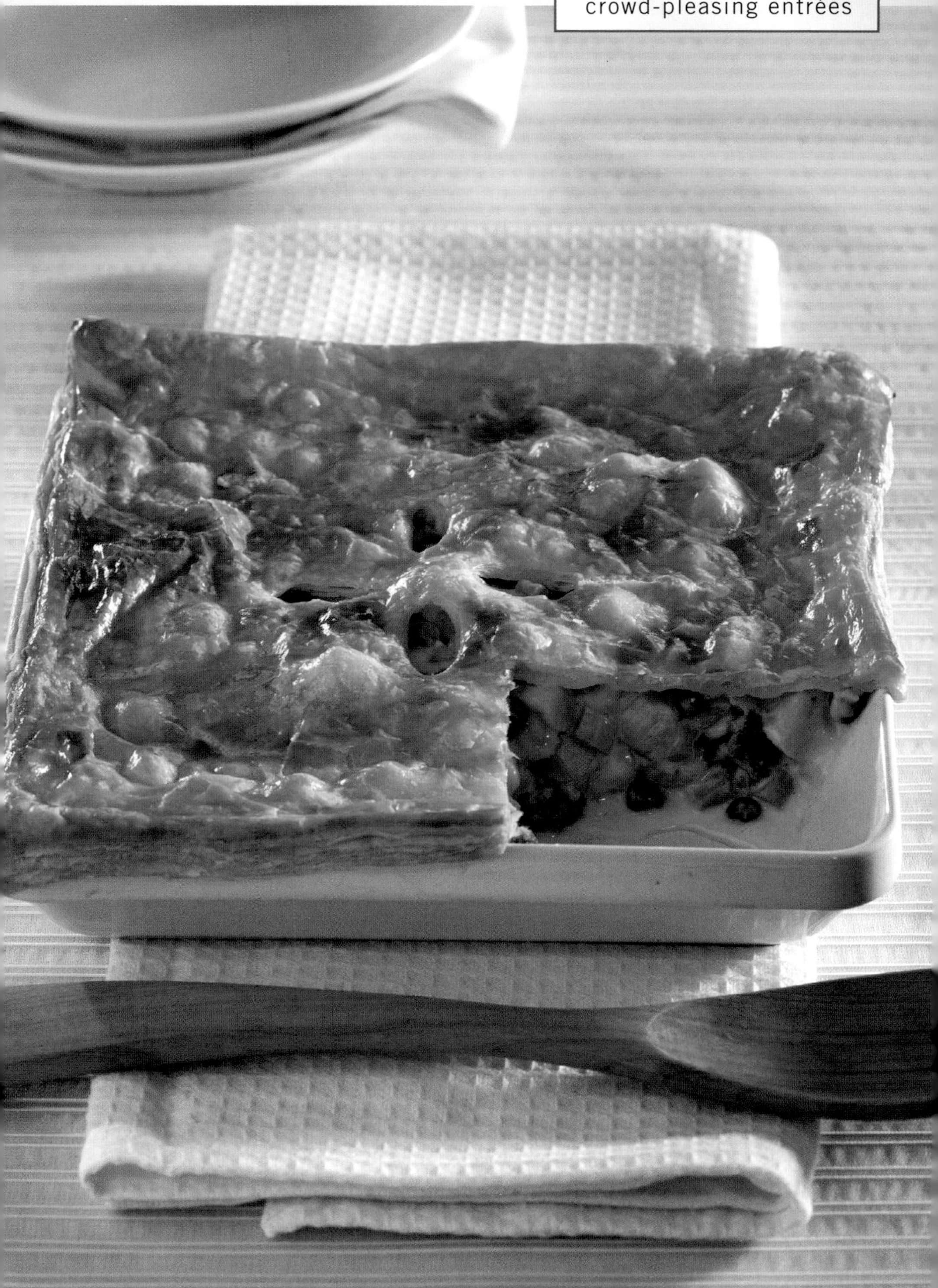

macaroni and cheese dijon

PREP: 20 min. | TOTAL: 45 min. | MAKES: 6 servings, 1 cup each.

▶ what you need!

1¼ cups milk

½ lb. (8 oz.) VELVEETA Pasteurized Prepared Cheese Product, cut into ½-inch cubes

2 Tbsp. GREY POUPON Dijon Mustard

3½ cups tri-colored rotini pasta, cooked, drained

6 slices OSCAR MAYER Bacon, cooked, crumbled

⅓ cup sliced green onions

⅛ tsp. ground red pepper (cayenne)

½ cup canned French fried onions

▶ make it!

1. **HEAT** oven to 350°F. Cook milk, VELVEETA and mustard in large saucepan on low heat until VELVEETA is completely melted and mixture is well blended, stirring occasionally. Add pasta, bacon, green onions and pepper; mix lightly.

2. **SPOON** into greased 2-qt. casserole; cover.

3. **BAKE** 15 to 20 min. or until heated through; stir. Top with onions. Bake, uncovered, 5 min. Let stand 10 min. before serving.

MAKE IT EASY:
For easy crumbled bacon, use kitchen scissors to snip raw bacon into ½-inch pieces. Let pieces fall right into skillet, then cook until crisp and drain on paper towels.

madras chicken

PREP: 15 min. | TOTAL: 35 min. | MAKES: 6 servings.

▶ what you need!

1 Tbsp. butter or margarine

½ cup chopped green peppers

½ cup chopped onions

1 clove garlic, minced

1 to 2 tsp. curry powder

1½ lb. boneless skinless chicken breasts, cut into bite-size pieces

1 can (14½ oz.) whole tomatoes, drained, cut up

1 tsp. lemon juice

½ tsp. dried thyme leaves

⅛ tsp. black pepper

½ lb. (8 oz.) VELVEETA Pasteurized Prepared Cheese Product, cut into ½-inch cubes

6 cups hot cooked rice

▶ make it!

1. **MELT** butter in large saucepan on medium heat. Add green peppers, onions, garlic and curry powder; cook and stir until vegetables are crisp-tender. Add chicken; cook and stir 5 min. or until no longer pink.

2. **STIR** in tomatoes, lemon juice, thyme and black pepper; simmer on low heat 5 min. or until chicken is done, stirring occasionally.

3. **ADD** VELVEETA; cook until melted, stirring frequently. Serve over rice.

USE YOUR MICROWAVE:
Combine green peppers, onions, garlic, curry powder and butter in 1½-qt. microwaveable casserole; cover. Microwave on HIGH 3 min. or until vegetables are crisp-tender. Add chicken; cover. Microwave 6 min. or until chicken is no longer pink, stirring after 3 min. Stir in tomatoes, lemon juice, thyme and black pepper. Microwave, covered, 2 min. or until chicken is done. Add VELVEETA. Microwave, covered, 1 min. or until VELVEETA is completely melted when stirred.

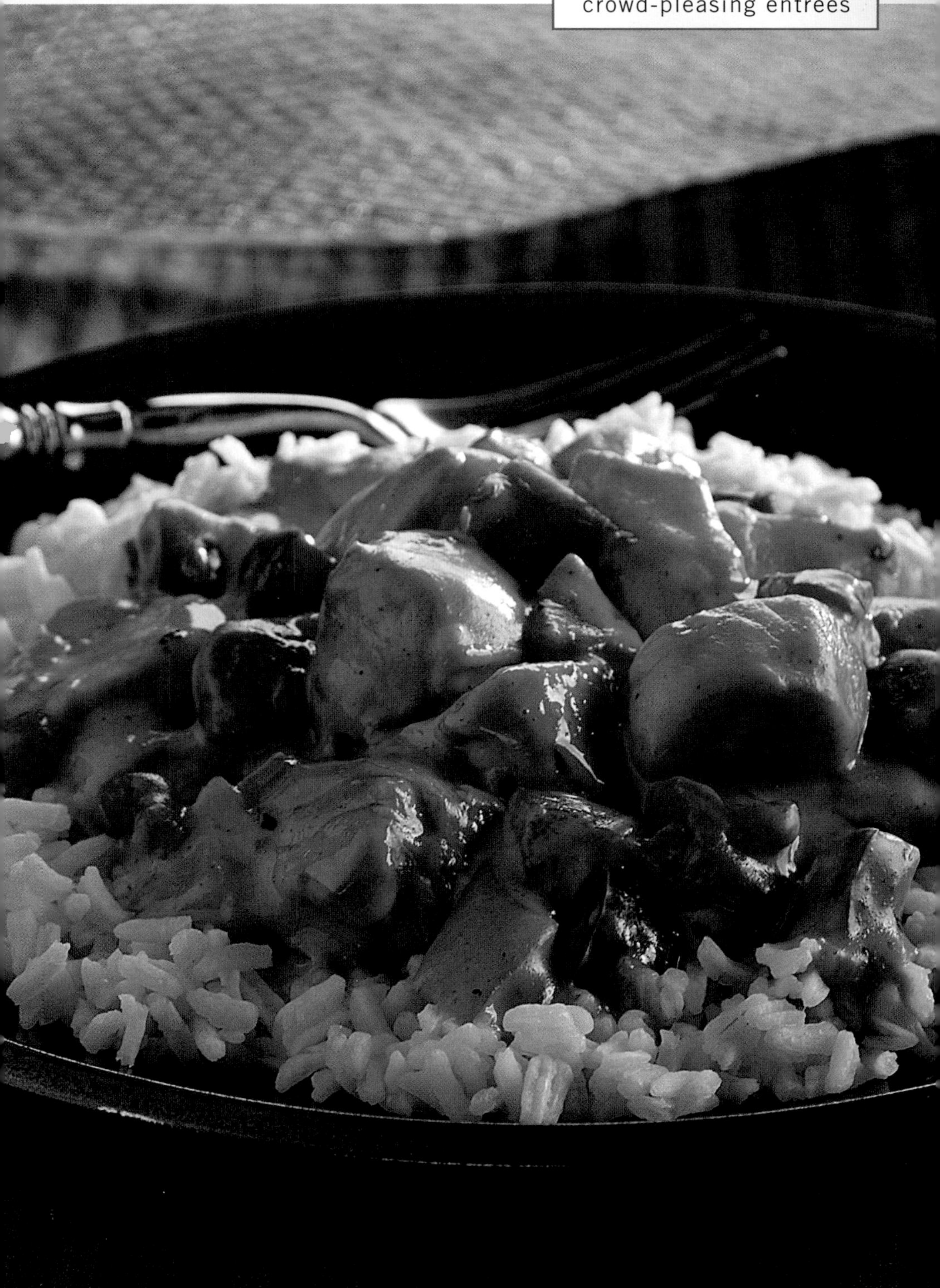

mexican tortilla stack

PREP: 15 min. | TOTAL: 45 min. | MAKES: 6 servings, 1¼ cups each.

▶ what you need!

1½ lb. lean ground beef

½ lb. (8 oz.) VELVEETA 2% Milk Pasteurized Prepared Cheese Product, cut into ½-inch cubes

3 cups frozen corn

1 jar (16 oz.) TACO BELL® HOME ORIGINALS® Thick 'N Chunky Medium Salsa

12 corn tortillas, cut into quarters

▶ make it!

1. **HEAT** oven to 400°F. Brown meat in large skillet; drain. Add VELVEETA; cook and stir until melted. Stir in corn and salsa.

2. **SPREAD** ¼ of meat mixture onto bottom of 13×9-inch baking dish; top with 16 tortilla pieces. Repeat layers 2 times. Top with remaining meat mixture; cover tightly with foil.

3. **BAKE** 30 min.

SPECIAL EXTRA:
Top each serving with 1 Tbsp. BREAKSTONE'S or KNUDSEN Sour Cream.

TACO BELL® and HOME ORIGINALS® are trademarks owned and licensed by Taco Bell Corp.

tuscan vegetable and sausage casserole

PREP: 25 min. | TOTAL: 1 hour 10 min. | MAKES: 8 servings, about 1¼ cups each.

► what you need!

4 cups penne pasta, cooked, drained

1 lb. Italian sausage, cut into ½-inch-thick slices

1 pkg. (16 oz.) frozen Italian-style vegetable combination

½ lb. (8 oz.) VELVEETA 2% Milk Pasteurized Prepared Cheese Product, cut into ½-inch cubes

1 jar (14 oz.) spaghetti sauce

⅓ cup milk

⅓ cup KRAFT Grated Parmesan Cheese

► make it!

1. HEAT oven to 400°F. Combine all ingredients except Parmesan in 13×9-inch baking dish; cover with foil.

2. BAKE 40 min. or until sausage is done and casserole is heated through; stir.

3. TOP with Parmesan.

GREAT LEFTOVERS:
Refrigerate any leftovers. To reheat, spoon 1⅓ cups pasta mixture onto microwaveable plate; cover with paper towel. Microwave on HIGH 2 to 2½ min. or until heated through. Repeat for additional servings as needed.

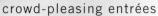

easy turkey divan

PREP: 10 min. | TOTAL: 35 min. | MAKES: 4 servings.

▶ what you need!

¼ lb. (4 oz.) VELVEETA Pasteurized Prepared Cheese Product, cut into ½-inch cubes

¼ cup MIRACLE WHIP Dressing

¼ cup milk

1 pkg. (10 oz.) frozen broccoli spears, cooked, drained

¾ lb. cooked turkey, cut into 4 slices

► make it!

1. **HEAT** oven to 350°F. Cook VELVEETA, dressing and milk in saucepan on low heat until VELVEETA is completely melted and mixture is well blended, stirring frequently.

2. **PLACE** broccoli in 10×6-inch baking dish; top with turkey and VELVEETA sauce.

3. **BAKE** 20 to 25 min. or until heated through.

   SUBSTITUTE:
   Substitute ham for the turkey.

67

VELVEETA bbq bacon cheeseburger mac

PREP: 10 min. | TOTAL: 25 min. | MAKES: 6 servings.

▶ what you need!

1½ lb. ground beef

1 small onion, chopped

2¾ cups water

½ cup BULL'S-EYE or KRAFT Original Barbecue Sauce

2 cups elbow macaroni, uncooked

½ lb. (8 oz.) VELVEETA Pasteurized Prepared Cheese Product, cut into ½-inch cubes

1 large tomato, chopped

½ cup OSCAR MAYER Bacon Pieces

▶ make it!

1. **BROWN** meat with onions in large skillet on medium heat; drain. Stir in water and barbecue sauce. Bring to boil. Add macaroni; cook 8 to 10 min. or until tender, stirring occasionally.

2. **STIR** in VELVEETA; cook until VELVEETA is completely melted and mixture is well blended, stirring occasionally.

3. **TOP** with tomatoes and bacon.

SERVING SUGGESTION:
Serve with a crisp green vegetable, such as hot steamed broccoli.

VELVEETA chicken enchilada casserole

PREP: 15 min. | TOTAL: 50 min. | MAKES: 6 servings.

▶ what you need!

¾ cup TACO BELL® HOME ORIGINALS® Thick 'N Chunky Salsa, divided

2 cups chopped cooked chicken

1 can (10¾ oz.) condensed cream of chicken soup

½ lb. (8 oz.) VELVEETA Mild Mexican Pasteurized Prepared Cheese Product with Jalapeño Peppers, cut into ½-inch cubes

6 corn tortillas (6 inch), cut in half

▶ make it!

1. **HEAT** oven to 350°F. Reserve ¼ cup salsa for later use. Mix chicken, soup and VELVEETA until well blended; spread 1 cup onto bottom of 8-inch square baking dish.

2. **TOP** with layers of 6 tortilla halves and ½ each of the remaining remaining salsa and chicken mixture; repeat layers.

3. **BAKE** 30 to 35 min. or until heated through. Serve topped with reserved salsa.

USE YOUR MICROWAVE:
Assemble as directed in 8-inch square microwaveable dish. Microwave on HIGH 10 to 14 min. or until heated through.

TACO BELL® and HOME ORIGINALS® are trademarks owned and licensed by Taco Bell Corp.

VELVEETA down-home macaroni & cheese

PREP: 20 min. | TOTAL: 40 min. | MAKES: 5 servings, 1 cup each.

▶ what you need!

¼ cup (½ stick) butter or margarine, divided

¼ cup flour

1 cup milk

½ lb. (8 oz.) VELVEETA Pasteurized Prepared Cheese Product, cut into ½-inch cubes

2 cups elbow macaroni, cooked, drained

½ cup KRAFT Shredded Cheddar Cheese

6 RITZ Crackers, crushed

▶ make it!

1. **HEAT** oven to 350°F. Melt 3 Tbsp. butter in medium saucepan on medium heat. Whisk in flour; cook 2 min., stirring constantly. Gradually stir in milk; cook until mixture boils and thickens, stirring constantly. Add VELVEETA; cook 3 min. or until melted, stirring frequently. Stir in macaroni.

2. **SPOON** into 2-qt. casserole sprayed with cooking spray; sprinkle with Cheddar. Melt remaining butter; toss with cracker crumbs. Sprinkle over casserole.

3. **BAKE** 20 min. or until heated through.

SPECIAL EXTRA:
Stir in ¼ cup OSCAR MAYER Real Bacon Bits with the cooked macaroni.

VELVEETA easy beef taco salad

PREP: 10 min. | TOTAL: 30 min. | MAKES: 6 servings, 1 cup each.

▶ what you need!

1 lb. ground beef

1 small onion, chopped

1 pkg. (1¼ oz.) TACO BELL® HOME ORIGINALS® Taco Seasoning Mix

¾ cup water

1 pkg. (10 oz.) frozen corn

½ lb. (8 oz.) VELVEETA Pasteurized Prepared Cheese Product, cut into ½-inch cubes

1 pkg. (8 oz.) shredded iceberg lettuce (about 4½ cups)

1 large tomato, chopped

6 oz. tortilla chips (about 9 cups)

▶ make it!

1. **COOK** meat and onions with seasoning mix and water in large skillet as directed on package.

2. **STIR** in corn and VELVEETA; cover. Cook on low heat 5 min. or until VELVEETA is completely melted and mixture is well blended, stirring frequently.

3. **SPOON** over lettuce just before serving; top with tomatoes. Serve with tortilla chips.

SIZE-WISE:
Let your kids help assemble these main-dish salads. As a bonus, they'll also learn about portion sizes.

TACO BELL® and HOME ORIGINALS® are trademarks owned and licensed by Taco Bell Corp.

VELVEETA italian sausage bake

PREP: 25 min. | TOTAL: 45 min. | MAKES: 6 servings, 1⅓ cups each.

▶ what you need!

1½ cups small penne pasta, uncooked

1 lb. Italian sausage, casings removed

4 small zucchini (10 oz.), halved lengthwise, sliced

1 red or green pepper, chopped

1 can (8 oz.) pizza sauce

½ lb. (8 oz.) VELVEETA Pasteurized Prepared Cheese Product, cut into
½-inch cubes

½ cup KRAFT Grated Parmesan Cheese

▶ make it!

1. HEAT oven to 350°F. Cook pasta as directed on package. Meanwhile, brown sausage in large deep skillet on medium-high heat, stirring occasionally to break up sausage. Drain; return sausage to skillet. Stir in zucchini, peppers and sauce; cook 5 to 6 min. or until vegetables are tender, stirring occasionally. Drain pasta. Add to sausage mixture along with VELVEETA; stir until well blended.

2. SPOON into 13×9-inch baking dish sprayed with cooking spray; sprinkle with Parmesan.

3. BAKE 15 to 20 min. or until heated through.

KID FRIENDLY:
Prepare as directed, substituting 1 lb. lean ground beef for the sausage and 1 cup each shredded carrots and zucchini for the 3 cups sliced zucchini. Also, try using a fun pasta shape, such as wagon wheels.

VELVEETA tex-mex beef and potatoes

PREP: 10 min. | TOTAL: 45 min. | MAKES: 6 servings, about 1⅓ cups each.

▶ what you need!

1 lb. ground beef

1 red pepper, chopped

1 onion, chopped

1 pkg. (1¼ oz.) TACO BELL® HOME ORIGINALS® Taco Seasoning Mix

½ cup water

4 cups frozen Southern-style hash browns (cubed not shredded variety)

1 pkg. (10 oz.) frozen corn

½ lb. (8 oz.) VELVEETA Pasteurized Prepared Cheese Product, cut into ½-inch cubes

▶ make it!

1.

2.

3.

HEAT oven to 350°F. Brown meat with peppers and onions in large skillet; drain. Return to skillet.

STIR in taco mix and water. Add potatoes, corn and VELVEETA; mix well. Spoon into 13×9-inch baking dish; cover with foil.

BAKE 20 min.; stir. Bake, uncovered, 15 min. or until heated through.

SIZE-WISE:
Need to feed a hungry family of 6? This tasty main dish can be on the table in a matter of minutes!

TACO BELL® and HOME ORIGINALS® are trademarks owned and licensed by Taco Bell Corp.

VELVEETA tuna noodle casserole

PREP: 20 min. | TOTAL: 55 min. | MAKES: 8 servings, about 1 cup each.

▶ what you need!

4 cups egg noodles, cooked, drained

1 pkg. (16 oz.) frozen peas and carrots

2 cans (6 oz. each) tuna, drained, flaked

1 can (10¾ oz.) condensed cream of mushroom soup

⅓ cup milk

¾ lb. (12 oz.) VELVEETA Pasteurized Prepared Cheese Product, cut into ½-inch cubes

1 can (2.8 oz.) French fried onion rings

▶ make it!

1. **HEAT** oven to 400°F. Combine all ingredients except onions in 13×9-inch baking dish; cover with foil.

2. **BAKE** 45 min. or until heated through; stir.

3. **TOP** with onions.

VARIATION:
Prepare using reduced-fat condensed cream of mushroom soup and VELVEETA 2% Milk Pasteurized Prepared Cheese Product.

soups & sandwiches

VELVEETA-bacon burgers

PREP: 10 min. | TOTAL: 24 min. | MAKES: 4 servings.

▶ what you need!

- 1 lb. extra-lean ground beef
- 2 Tbsp. KRAFT Light House Italian Dressing
- ¼ lb. (4 oz.) VELVEETA 2% Milk Pasteurized Prepared Cheese Product, cut into 4 slices
- 4 tsp. OSCAR MAYER Bacon Pieces
- 4 whole wheat hamburger buns

▶ make it!

1. **SHAPE** meat into 4 patties. Cook in dressing in skillet on medium-high heat 10 to 12 min. or until done (160°F), turning after 5 min.

2. **TOP** with VELVEETA and bacon; cover. Cook 1 to 2 min. or until VELVEETA begins to melt.

3. **SERVE** in buns.

SPECIAL EXTRA:
Cover bottom half of each bun with lettuce leaf before topping with burger.

beef wrap melt

PREP: 5 min. | TOTAL: 6 min. | MAKES: 1 serving.

▶ what you need!

- 1 tsp. KRAFT Light Mayo Reduced Fat Mayonnaise
- 1 tsp. KRAFT Prepared Horseradish
- 1 whole wheat tortilla (8 inch)
- 6 slices OSCAR MAYER Deli Fresh Shaved Roast Beef
- 1 slice VELVEETA 2% Milk Pasteurized Prepared Cheese Product (½ oz.)
- 12 baby spinach leaves
- 2 Tbsp. chopped tomatoes

▶ make it!

1. **MIX** mayo and horseradish; spread onto tortilla.

2. **TOP** with remaining ingredients; roll up, or fold tortilla in half as preferred. Place on microwaveable plate.

3. **MICROWAVE** on HIGH 1 min. or until VELVEETA is melted.

SUBSTITUTE:
Omit mayo. Substitute KRAFT Horseradish Sauce for the prepared horseradish.

cheesy chicken ranch sandwiches

PREP: 10 min. | TOTAL: 24 min. | MAKES: 6 servings.

▶ what you need!

6 small boneless skinless chicken breast halves (1½ lb.)

⅔ cup KRAFT Ranch Dressing, divided

6 oz. VELVEETA Pasteurized Prepared Cheese Product, cut into 6 slices

6 French bread rolls, split

6 large lettuce leaves

▶ make it!

1. **HEAT** broiler. Place chicken on rack of broiler pan sprayed with cooking spray. Brush with ⅓ cup dressing.

2. **BROIL**, 3 to 4 inches from heat, 5 to 6 min. on each side or until chicken is done (165°F). Top with VELVEETA; broil 2 min. or until melted.

3. **SPREAD** rolls with remaining dressing; fill with lettuce and chicken.

SERVING SUGGESTION:
Serve with your favorite fresh fruit.

cheesy spinach soup

PREP: 15 min. | TOTAL: 25 min. | MAKES: 4 servings, about 1 cup each.

► what you need!

1 Tbsp. soft reduced calorie margarine

¼ cup chopped onions

2 cups fat-free milk

½ lb. (8 oz.) VELVEETA 2% Milk Pasteurized Prepared Cheese Product, cut into ½-inch cubes

1 pkg. (10 oz.) frozen chopped spinach, cooked, well drained

⅛ tsp. ground nutmeg

dash pepper

► make it!

1. **MELT** margarine in medium saucepan on medium heat. Add onions; cook and stir until tender.

2. **ADD** remaining ingredients; cook on low heat until VELVEETA is melted and soup is heated through, stirring occasionally.

SIZE-WISE:
Savor the flavor of this cheesy soup while keeping portion size in mind.

cheesy turkey grill

PREP: 5 min. | TOTAL: 11 min. | MAKES: 4 servings.

▶ what you need!

8 slices whole wheat bread

2 oz. VELVEETA 2% Milk Pasteurized Prepared Cheese Product, cut into 4 slices

16 slices OSCAR MAYER Deli Fresh Shaved Oven Roasted Turkey Breast

1 Tbsp. margarine, softened

▶ make it!

1. **FILL** bread slices with VELVEETA and turkey.

2. **SPREAD** outsides of sandwiches with margarine.

3. **COOK** in large skillet on medium heat 3 min. on each side or until golden brown on both sides.

SPECIAL EXTRA:
Spread bread with GREY POUPON Dijon Mustard before filling with the VELVEETA and turkey.

VELVEETA sweet & cheesy panini

PREP: **10** min. | TOTAL: **16** min. | MAKES: **4** servings.

▶ what you need!

8 slices bread

¼ lb. (4 oz.) VELVEETA Pasteurized Prepared Cheese Product, cut into 8 slices

24 slices OSCAR MAYER Deli Fresh Shaved Brown Sugar Ham

1 Granny Smith apple, thinly sliced

8 tsp. margarine, softened

2 tsp. powdered sugar

▶ make it!

1. **FILL** bread slices with VELVEETA, ham and apples.

2. **SPREAD** outsides of sandwiches with margarine.

3. **COOK** in skillet on medium heat 3 min. on each side or until golden brown on both sides. Sprinkle with powdered sugar.

SERVING SUGGESTION:
Serve with a tossed green salad topped with your favorite KRAFT Light Dressing, such as Ranch.

quick bacon & "egg-wich"

PREP: 1 min. | TOTAL: 2 min. 10 sec. | MAKES: 1 serving.

► what you need!

1 whole wheat English muffin, split

1 egg

1 thin slice tomato

1 slice OSCAR MAYER Fully Cooked Bacon, cut in half

1 slice VELVEETA 2% Milk Pasteurized Prepared Cheese Product (½ oz.)

► make it!

1. **PLACE** 1 English muffin half on microwaveable plate. Carefully crack egg over muffin. Microwave on HIGH 40 sec.

2. **TOP** with tomato, bacon and VELVEETA; cover with remaining muffin half.

3. **MICROWAVE** on HIGH 30 sec. or until egg white is completely set and yolk is thickened around the edge.

TAKE ALONG:
Wrap hot sandwich in foil before heading out the door to enjoy as part of a quick grab-'n'-go breakfast.

santa fe chicken fajita soup

PREP: 15 min. | TOTAL: 1 hour 5 min. (incl. refrigerating) | MAKES: 8 servings, 1 cup each.

▶ what you need!

1 pkg. (1.4 oz.) TACO BELL® HOME ORIGINALS® Fajita Seasoning Mix

⅓ cup water

1 lb. boneless skinless chicken breasts, cut into thin strips

4 large cloves garlic, minced

2 Tbsp. chopped fresh cilantro

1 large red onion, chopped

1 small green pepper, chopped

1 pkg. (8 oz.) PHILADELPHIA Fat Free Cream Cheese, cut into cubes

1 lb. (16 oz.) VELVEETA 2% Milk Pasteurized Prepared Cheese Product, cut into ½-inch cubes

2 cans (14.5 oz. each) fat-free reduced-sodium chicken broth

▶ make it!

1. **COMBINE** seasoning mix and water in medium bowl. Add chicken; toss to evenly coat. Refrigerate 30 min.

2. **COOK** garlic and cilantro in large nonstick saucepan sprayed with cooking spray on medium-high heat 1 min. Stir in chicken mixture, onions and peppers; cook 10 min. or until chicken is done, stirring frequently.

3. **ADD** cream cheese, VELVEETA and broth; mix well. Cook on medium heat until cream cheese and VELVEETA are completely melted and chicken mixture is heated through, stirring occasionally.

SERVING SUGGESTION:
Serve this hearty main-dish soup with a tossed leafy green salad.

TACO BELL® and HOME ORIGINALS® are trademarks owned and licensed by Taco Bell Corp.

southwest chicken pita

PREP: 5 min. | TOTAL: 15 min. | MAKES: 1 serving

▶ what you need!

- 2 Tbsp. chopped red peppers
- 1 Tbsp. KRAFT Mayo Fat Free Mayonnaise Dressing
- 2 tsp. BULL'S-EYE Smokin' Chipotle Barbecue Sauce
- ½ cup OSCAR MAYER Deli Fresh Oven Roasted Chicken Breast Cuts
- ½ whole wheat pita bread
- 1 slice VELVEETA 2% Milk Pasteurized Prepared Cheese Product (½ oz.)

▶ make it!

1. **HEAT** oven to 350°F. Mix peppers, dressing and sauce in small bowl. Add chicken; toss to coat.

2. **FILL** pita half with VELVEETA and chicken mixture. Wrap in foil.

3. **BAKE** 10 min. or until sandwich is heated through and VELVEETA is melted.

CREATIVE LEFTOVERS:
This is a great way to use leftover cooked chicken.

southwestern corn soup

PREP: 10 min. | TOTAL: 25 min. | MAKES: 6 servings, ¾ cup each.

▶ what you need!

¾ cup chopped green peppers

1 Tbsp. butter or margarine

3 oz. PHILADELPHIA Cream Cheese, cubed

½ lb. (8 oz.) VELVEETA Mexican Pasteurized Prepared Cheese Product, cut into ½-inch cubes

1 can (14.75 oz.) cream-style corn

1½ cups milk

¼ cup crushed tortilla chips

▶ make it!

1. **COOK** and stir peppers in butter in medium saucepan on medium heat until crisp-tender.

2. **ADD** cream cheese; cook on low heat until melted, stirring frequently. Stir in VELVEETA, corn and milk; cook until VELVEETA is completely melted and soup is heated through, stirring occasionally.

3. **SERVE** topped with chips.

SPECIAL EXTRA:
Garnish with chopped cilantro for a burst of extra-fresh flavor.

turkey-cheese pita

PREP: **10** min. | TOTAL: **18** min. | MAKES: **4** servings.

▶ what you need!

4 whole wheat pita breads

2 tsp. GREY POUPON Hearty Spicy Brown Mustard

16 baby spinach leaves

¼ lb. (4 oz.) VELVEETA 2% Milk Pasteurized Prepared Cheese Product, sliced, cut into strips

1 pkg. (6 oz.) OSCAR MAYER Thin Sliced Oven Roasted Turkey Breast, cut into strips

½ cup sliced fresh mushrooms

½ cup slivered red onions

▶ make it!

1. **SPREAD** bread with mustard; top with remaining ingredients.

2. **MICROWAVE**, 1 at a time, on microwaveable plate on HIGH 1 to 2 min. or until VELVEETA begins to melt.

FUN IDEA:
Top pitas as directed; roll up, then tie closed with green onion top.

VELVEETA salsa joe sandwich

PREP: 10 min. | TOTAL: 25 min. | MAKES: 6 servings.

▶ what you need!

1 lb. lean ground beef

¼ cup chopped onions

6 oz. VELVEETA Pasteurized Prepared Cheese Product, cut into ½-inch cubes

1 cup TACO BELL® HOME ORIGINALS® Thick 'N Chunky Salsa

6 kaiser rolls, partially split

▶ make it!

1. **BROWN** meat with onions in large skillet on medium heat; drain. Return to skillet.

2. **STIR** in VELVEETA and salsa; cook on medium-low heat until VELVEETA is completely melted and mixture is well blended, stirring frequently.

3. **SPOON** into rolls just before serving.

VELVEETA CHEESY TACOS:
Omit rolls. Prepare meat mixture as directed; spoon into 12 TACO BELL® HOME ORIGINALS® Taco Shells. Top with shredded lettuce and chopped tomatoes. Makes 6 servings, 2 tacos each.

TACO BELL® and HOME ORIGINALS® are trademarks owned and licensed by Taco Bell Corp.

VELVEETA ultimate grilled cheese

PREP: 5 min. | TOTAL: 11 min. | MAKES: 4 servings.

▶ what you need!

8 slices white bread

6 oz. VELVEETA Pasteurized Prepared Cheese Product, sliced

8 tsp. soft margarine

▶ make it!

1. **FILL** bread slices with VELVEETA.

2. **SPREAD** outsides of sandwiches with margarine.

3. **COOK** in skillet on medium heat 3 min. on each side or until golden brown on both sides.

SUBSTITUTE:
Prepare using VELVEETA 2% Milk Pasteurized Prepared Cheese Product.

VELVEETA wow! burger

PREP: **10 min.** | TOTAL: **30 min.** | MAKES: **6 servings.**

▶ what you need!

| 1½ lb. extra lean ground beef | 6 oz. VELVEETA 2% Milk Pasteurized Prepared Cheese Product, cut into 6 slices | 6 whole wheat hamburger buns, toasted | 1 can (10 oz.) RO*TEL Diced Tomatoes & Green Chilies, drained |

▶ make it!

1. **HEAT** grill to medium heat. Shape meat into 6 (¾-inch-thick) patties.

2. **GRILL** 7 to 9 min. on each side or until done (160°F). Top with VELVEETA; grill 1 to 2 min. or until melted.

3. **PLACE** cheeseburgers on bottom halves of buns; cover with tomatoes and tops of buns.

SERVING SUGGESTION:
Serve with fresh fruit and assorted cut-up fresh vegetables to round out the meal.

HOW TO USE YOUR STOVE:
Cook patties in skillet on medium heat 4 to 6 min. on each side or until done (160°F). Top with VELVEETA; cover with lid. Cook 1 to 2 min. or until VELVEETA is melted. Continue as directed.

*Ro*Tel is a product of ConAgra Foods, Inc.*

appetizers, snacks & sides

VELVEETA double-decker nachos

PREP: 15 min. | TOTAL: 15 min. | MAKES: 6 servings.

▶ what you need!

- 6 oz. tortilla chips (about 7 cups)
- 1 can (15 oz.) chili with beans
- ½ lb. (8 oz.) VELVEETA Pasteurized Prepared Cheese Product, cut into ½-inch cubes
- 1 tomato, finely chopped
- 2 green onions, sliced
- ⅓ cup BREAKSTONE'S or KNUDSEN Sour Cream

▶ make it!

1. **ARRANGE** ½ of the chips on large microwaveable platter; top with layers of ½ each of the chili and VELVEETA. Repeat layers.

2. **MICROWAVE** on HIGH 3 to 5 min. or until VELVEETA is melted.

3. **TOP** with remaining ingredients.

SIZE-WISE:
Enjoy your favorite foods while keeping portion size in mind.

5-minute cheesy broccoli toss

PREP: 5 min. | TOTAL: 10 min. | MAKES: 4 servings, about ¾ cup each.

▶ what you need!

4 cups frozen broccoli florets

½ tsp. dry mustard

¼ lb. (4 oz.) VELVEETA Pasteurized Prepared Cheese Product, cut into
½-inch cubes

1 Tbsp. KRAFT Grated Parmesan Cheese

▶ make it!

1. **COMBINE** broccoli, mustard and VELVEETA in large nonstick skillet on
medium-high heat.

2. **COOK** 5 min. or until broccoli is crisp-tender and mixture is heated
through, stirring occasionally.

3. **SPRINKLE** with Parmesan.

SPECIAL EXTRA:
Add 1 minced garlic clove with the broccoli.

bacon-spinach bites

PREP: 10 min. | TOTAL: 30 min. | MAKES: 12 servings.

▶ what you need!

4 oz. (½ of 8-oz. pkg.) PHILADELPHIA Cream Cheese, softened

4 green onions, sliced

1 pkg. (10 oz.) frozen chopped spinach, thawed, squeezed dry

6 slices OSCAR MAYER Bacon, cooked, crumbled

3 Tbsp. flour

4 eggs, beaten

¼ lb. (4 oz.) VELVEETA Pasteurized Prepared Cheese Product, cut into 12 cubes

▶ make it!

1. **HEAT** oven to 350°F. Mix cream cheese and onions in medium bowl. Add spinach, bacon and flour; mix well. Stir in eggs.

2. **SPOON** into 12 greased and floured muffin pan cups. Top each with 1 VELVEETA cube; press gently into center of filling.

3. **BAKE** 20 min. or until centers are set and tops are golden brown. Serve warm or chilled.

MINIATURE BACON-SPINACH BITES:
Prepare spinach mixture as directed; spoon into 24 greased and floured miniature muffin pan cups. Cut VELVEETA into 24 cubes; press 1 into batter in each cup. Bake 14 to 16 min. or until centers are set and tops are golden brown. Makes 12 servings, 2 appetizers each.

cheesy chipotle vegetable bake

PREP: 15 min. | TOTAL: 50 min. | MAKES: 10 servings, ¾ cup each.

▶ what you need!

4 cups small cauliflower florets

4 large zucchini, sliced

3 carrots, sliced

2 Tbsp. chopped chipotle peppers in adobo sauce

¼ cup KRAFT Zesty Italian Dressing

½ lb. (8 oz.) VELVEETA Pasteurized Prepared Cheese Product, thinly sliced

20 RITZ Crackers, crushed

2 Tbsp. butter or margarine, melted

▶ make it!

1. **HEAT** oven to 375°F. Combine first 5 ingredients; spoon into 13×9-inch baking dish. Top with VELVEETA.

2. **MIX** cracker crumbs and butter; sprinkle over vegetable mixture.

3. **BAKE** 30 to 35 min. or until vegetables are tender and casserole is heated through.

MAKE AHEAD:
Assemble casserole as directed. Store in refrigerator until ready to bake as directed.

cheesy potato skins

PREP: 15 min. | TOTAL: 43 min. | MAKES: 16 servings.

▶ what you need!

4 large baked potatoes (2½ lb.)

2 Tbsp. butter or margarine, melted

¼ lb. (4 oz.) VELVEETA Pasteurized Prepared Cheese Product, cut into ½-inch cubes

2 Tbsp. chopped red peppers

2 slices OSCAR MAYER Bacon, cooked, crumbled

1 Tbsp. sliced green onions

▶ make it!

1. **HEAT** oven to 450°F. Cut potatoes in half lengthwise; scoop out centers, leaving ¼-inch-thick shells. (Refrigerate removed potato centers for another use.) Cut shells crosswise in half. Place, skin-sides down, on baking sheet; brush with butter.

2. **BAKE** 20 to 25 min. or until crisp and golden brown.

3. **FILL** shells with VELVEETA; continue baking until VELVEETA begins to melt. Top with remaining ingredients.

HOW TO BAKE POTATOES:
Russet potatoes are the best for baking. Scrub potatoes well, blot dry and rub the skin with a little oil and salt. Prick the skin of the potatoes with a fork so steam can escape. Stand them on end in a muffin tin. Bake at 425°F for 45 min. to 1 hour or until tender.

crispy tostadas

PREP: 10 min. | TOTAL: 17 min. | MAKES: 8 servings.

▶ what you need!

8 tostada shells (5 inch)

1 can (16 oz.) TACO BELL® HOME ORIGINALS® Refried Beans

1 cup finely chopped mixed red and green peppers

½ lb. (8 oz.) VELVEETA Pepper Jack Pasteurized Prepared Cheese Product, sliced

1 cup shredded lettuce

½ cup TACO BELL® HOME ORIGINALS® Thick 'N Chunky Salsa

▶ make it!

1. **HEAT** oven to 350°F. Spread tostada shells with beans; top with peppers and VELVEETA.

2. **BAKE** 5 to 7 min. or until filling is heated through and VELVEETA is melted.

3. **TOP** with lettuce and salsa.

CRISPY BEEF TOSTADAS:
Omit beans. Cook 1 lb. lean ground beef with 1 pkg. (1¼ oz.) TACO BELL® HOME ORIGINALS® Taco Seasoning Mix as directed on package. Spoon into tostada shells; top with peppers and VELVEETA. Continue as directed.

TACO BELL® and HOME ORIGINALS® are trademarks owned and licensed by Taco Bell Corp.

easy cheesy mashed potatoes

PREP: 25 min. | TOTAL: 25 min. | MAKES: 8 servings, about ½ cup each.

▶ what you need!

2 lb. Yukon gold potatoes (about 5), cubed

¼ cup milk

2 oz. VELVEETA Pasteurized Prepared Cheese Product, cut into ½-inch cubes

¼ tsp. garlic powder

1 green onion, thinly sliced

▶ make it!

1. **COOK** potatoes in large saucepan of boiling water 15 min. or until tender. Drain potatoes; return to saucepan.

2. **MASH** potatoes until light and fluffy, gradually adding milk alternately with the VELVEETA.

3. **STIR** in garlic powder. Top with onions.

SPECIAL EXTRA:
For a change of pace, stir ¼ cup OSCAR MAYER Real Bacon Bits into mashed potatoes with garlic powder.

easy cheesy potatoes

PREP: 15 min. | TOTAL: 1 hour 10 min. | MAKES: 10 servings, ½ cup each.

▶ what you need!

1 lb. russet potatoes (about 4 medium), cut into ½-inch chunks

½ lb. (8 oz.) VELVEETA Pasteurized Prepared Cheese Product, cut up

½ cup chopped onions

¼ cup KRAFT Real Mayo Mayonnaise

4 slices OSCAR MAYER Bacon, cooked, drained and crumbled (about ¼ cup)

▶ make it!

1. **HEAT** oven to 375°F. Combine all ingredients except bacon in 8-inch square baking dish sprayed with cooking spray; cover with foil.

2. **BAKE** 45 min.

3. **TOP** with bacon; bake, uncovered, 5 to 10 min. or until potatoes are tender.

SPECIAL EXTRA:
Sprinkle with 1 Tbsp. chopped fresh parsley just before serving.

make-ahead broccoli, cheese & rice

PREP: 10 min. | TOTAL: 20 min. | MAKES: 12 servings, ½ cup each.

▶ what you need!

- 6 cups fresh broccoli florets
- 1 can (14½ oz.) fat-free reduced-sodium chicken broth
- 2 cups instant white rice, uncooked
- ½ lb. (8 oz.) VELVEETA Pasteurized Prepared Cheese Product, cut into ½-inch cubes
- 1½ Tbsp. butter
- 10 RITZ Crackers, crushed
- 2 Tbsp. KRAFT Grated Parmesan Cheese

▶ make it!

1.

BRING broccoli and broth to boil in medium saucepan on medium-high heat. Stir in rice; cover. Remove from heat. Let stand 5 min. Stir in VELVEETA. Let stand, covered, 5 min. Stir until VELVEETA is completely melted. Spoon into microwaveable bowl; cover with plastic wrap. Refrigerate up to 24 hours.

2.

MEANWHILE, melt butter in small skillet on medium heat. Add cracker crumbs; cook 2 to 3 min. or until golden brown, stirring frequently. Cool completely. Stir in Parmesan; spoon into resealable plastic bag. Seal bag. Store at room temperature up to 24 hours.

3.

COVER broccoli mixture with waxed paper. Microwave on HIGH 5 to 6 min. or until broccoli mixture is heated through; stir. Sprinkle with crumb mixture. Microwave, uncovered, 2 to 3 min. or until heated through.

VARIATION:
Prepare using fat-free reduced-sodium chicken broth and VELVEETA 2% Milk Pasteurized Prepared Cheese Product.

new-look scalloped potatoes and ham

PREP: 30 min. | TOTAL: 1 hour | MAKES: 16 servings, about 1 cup each.

▶ what you need!

4½ lb. red potatoes (about 9), cut into ¼-inch-thick slices

1 container (16 oz.) BREAKSTONE'S FREE or KNUDSEN FREE Fat Free Sour Cream

¾ lb. (12 oz.) VELVEETA 2% Milk Pasteurized Prepared Cheese Product, cut into ½-inch cubes

8 oz. (½ of 1-lb. pkg.) OSCAR MAYER Smoked Ham, chopped

4 green onions, sliced

¼ cup KRAFT Grated Parmesan Cheese

▶ make it!

1. **HEAT** oven to 350°F. Cook potatoes in boiling water in large covered saucepan 10 to 12 min. or just until potatoes are tender; drain. Remove ¾ of the potatoes; place in large bowl. Add sour cream; mash until smooth. Stir in VELVEETA, ham and onions. Add remaining potato slices; stir gently.

2. **SPOON** into 13×9-inch baking dish sprayed with cooking spray; sprinkle with Parmesan.

3. **BAKE** 30 min. or until heated through.

PURCHASING POTATOES:
Look for firm, smooth, well-shaped potatoes that are free of wrinkles, cracks and blemishes. Avoid any with green-tinged skins or sprouting "eyes" or buds.

130

speedy spicy quesadillas

PREP: 5 min. | TOTAL: 8 min. | MAKES: 8 servings.

▶ what you need!

½ lb. (8 oz.) VELVEETA Mexican Pasteurized Prepared Cheese Product, cut into 8 slices

8 flour tortillas (6 inch)

▶ make it!

1. **PLACE** 1 VELVEETA slice on bottom half of each tortilla; fold in half. Place 2 tortillas on microwaveable plate.

2. **MICROWAVE** on HIGH 30 to 45 sec. or until VELVEETA is melted. Repeat with remaining tortillas.

3. **CUT** in half to serve.

SPECIAL EXTRA:
Garnish with chopped fresh tomatoes and green onions.

vegetables in cream sauce

PREP: 10 min. | TOTAL: 23 min. | MAKES: 6 servings, ½ cup each.

▶ what you need!

1 pkg. (16 oz.) frozen broccoli, cauliflower and carrot blend

¼ lb. (4 oz.) VELVEETA 2% Milk Pasteurized Prepared Cheese Product, cut into ½-inch cubes

4 oz. (½ of 8-oz. pkg.) PHILADELPHIA ⅓ Less Fat Cream Cheese, cubed

▶ make it!

1. LAYER ingredients in microwaveable 1½-qt. casserole; cover.

2. MICROWAVE on HIGH 13 min. or until vegetables are heated through, stirring after 7 min.; stir.

USE YOUR OVEN:
Heat oven to 350°F. Layer ingredients in 1-qt. casserole as directed. Bake 55 min. or until vegetables are heated through; stir.

VELVEETA classic potatoes au gratin

PREP: 15 min. | TOTAL: 40 min. | MAKES: 8 servings, about ½ cup each.

▶ what you need!

1½ lb. potatoes (about 3 large), thinly sliced

½ lb. (8 oz.) VELVEETA 2% Milk Pasteurized Prepared Cheese Product, cut into ½-inch cubes

½ cup chopped onions

¼ cup milk

1 tsp. dry mustard

½ tsp. black pepper

▶ make it!

1. **COOK** potatoes in boiling water in large saucepan 8 to 10 min. or just until tender; drain.

2. **HEAT** oven to 350°F. Toss potatoes with remaining ingredients in 2-qt. casserole; cover with lid.

3. **BAKE** 22 to 25 min. or until potatoes are tender. Stir gently before serving.

SERVING SUGGESTION:
Add contrast to the potatoes by adding a crisp mixed green salad alongside cooked lean fish, meat or poultry.

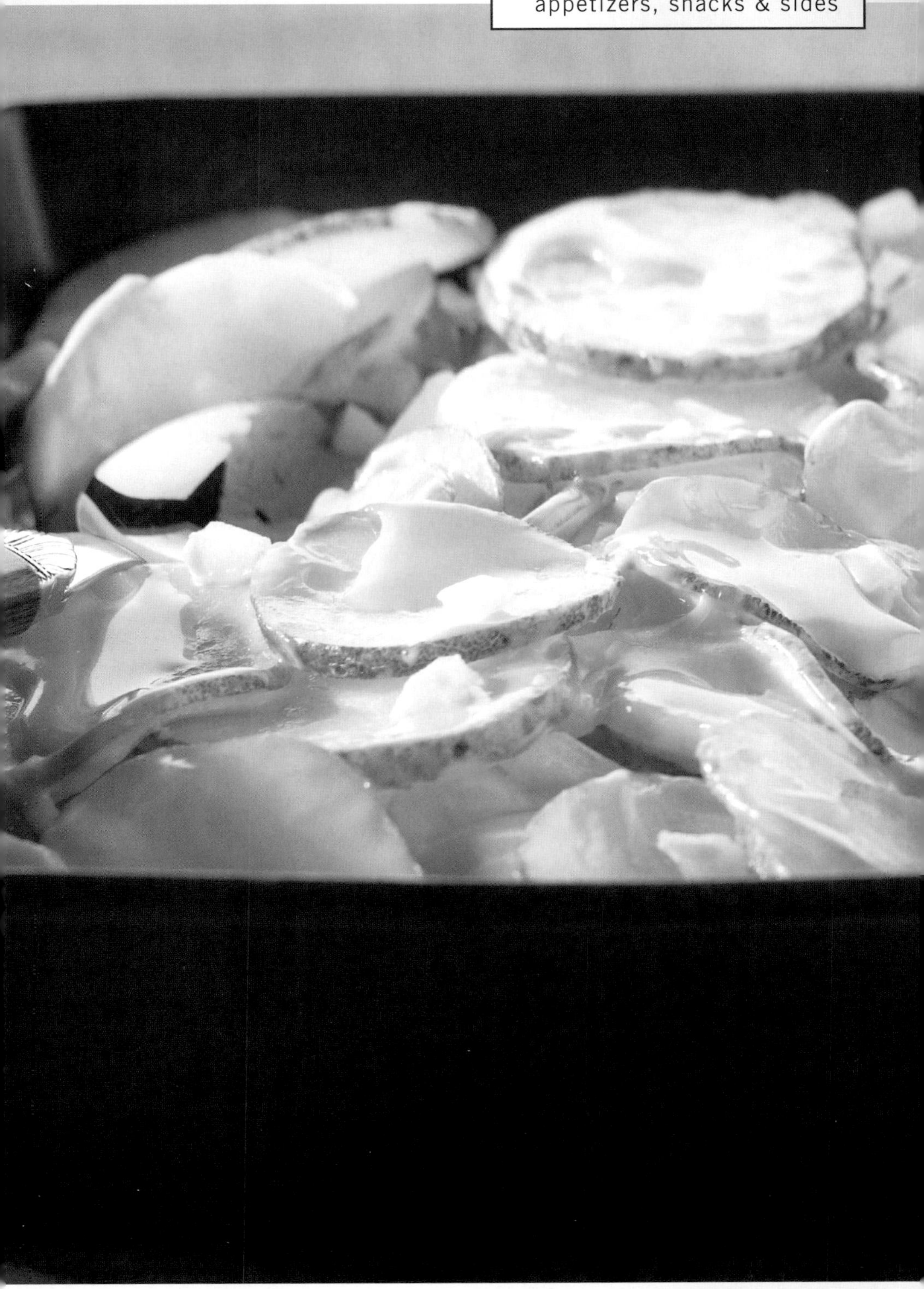

cheesy scramblin' pizza

PREP: 10 min. | TOTAL: 20 min. | MAKES: 8 servings.

▶ what you need!

6 eggs

¼ cup milk

2 green onions, sliced

1 small tomato, chopped

1 Italian pizza crust (12 inch)

½ lb. (8 oz.) VELVEETA Pasteurized Prepared Cheese Product, cut into ½-inch cubes

6 slices OSCAR MAYER Fully Cooked Bacon, cut into 1-inch pieces

▶ make it!

1. HEAT oven to 450°F. Beat eggs, milk, onions and tomatoes with whisk until well blended. Pour into nonstick skillet sprayed with cooking spray; cook on medium-low heat until eggs are set, stirring occasionally.

2. PLACE crust on baking sheet; top with egg mixture, VELVEETA and bacon.

3. BAKE 10 min. or until VELVEETA is melted.

SERVING SUGGESTION:
For a delightful brunch idea, serve with a seasonal fresh fruit salad.

fresh vegetable medley

PREP: 10 min. | TOTAL: 25 min. | MAKES: 12 servings, about ½ cup each.

▶ what you need!

1 small onion, chopped

1 Tbsp. margarine

½ lb. (8 oz.) VELVEETA Pasteurized Prepared Cheese Product, cut into ½-inch cubes

1 can (10¾ oz.) condensed cream of mushroom soup

8 cups mixed fresh vegetables (broccoli and cauliflower florets; sliced carrots, squash and zucchini; cut-up green beans; corn)

▶ make it!

1. **COOK** and stir onions in margarine in large skillet on medium heat until crisp-tender.

2. **ADD** VELVEETA and soup; cook until VELVEETA is completely melted and mixture is well blended, stirring frequently.

3. **STIR** in remaining vegetables; cook 10 min. or until crisp-tender, stirring frequently.

SHORTCUT:
To shave even more time off this easy recipe, purchase cut-up fresh vegetables from the supermarket salad bar. Or, substitute 2 pkg. (16 oz. each) frozen mixed vegetables for the 8 cups mixed fresh vegetables.

143

VOLUME MEASUREMENTS (dry)

$1/8$ teaspoon = 0.5 mL
$1/4$ teaspoon = 1 mL
$1/2$ teaspoon = 2 mL
$3/4$ teaspoon = 4 mL
1 teaspoon = 5 mL
1 tablespoon = 15 mL
2 tablespoons = 30 mL
$1/4$ cup = 60 mL
$1/3$ cup = 75 mL
$1/2$ cup = 125 mL
$2/3$ cup = 150 mL
$3/4$ cup = 175 mL
1 cup = 250 mL
2 cups = 1 pint = 500 mL
3 cups = 750 mL
4 cups = 1 quart = 1 L

VOLUME MEASUREMENTS (fluid)

1 fluid ounce (2 tablespoons) = 30 mL
4 fluid ounces ($1/2$ cup) = 125 mL
8 fluid ounces (1 cup) = 250 mL
12 fluid ounces ($1 1/2$ cups) = 375 mL
16 fluid ounces (2 cups) = 500 mL

WEIGHTS (mass)

$1/2$ ounce = 15 g
1 ounce = 30 g
3 ounces = 90 g
4 ounces = 120 g
8 ounces = 225 g
10 ounces = 285 g
12 ounces = 360 g
16 ounces = 1 pound = 450 g

DIMENSIONS

$1/16$ inch = 2 mm
$1/8$ inch = 3 mm
$1/4$ inch = 6 mm
$1/2$ inch = 1.5 cm
$3/4$ inch = 2 cm
1 inch = 2.5 cm

OVEN TEMPERATURES

250°F = 120°C
275°F = 140°C
300°F = 150°C
325°F = 160°C
350°F = 180°C
375°F = 190°C
400°F = 200°C
425°F = 220°C
450°F = 230°C

BAKING PAN SIZES

Utensil	Size in Inches/Quarts	Metric Volume	Size in Centimeters
Baking or	$8 \times 8 \times 2$	2 L	$20 \times 20 \times 5$
Cake Pan	$9 \times 9 \times 2$	2.5 L	$23 \times 23 \times 5$
(square or	$12 \times 8 \times 2$	3 L	$30 \times 20 \times 5$
rectangular)	$13 \times 9 \times 2$	3.5 L	$33 \times 23 \times 5$
Loaf Pan	$8 \times 4 \times 3$	1.5 L	$20 \times 10 \times 7$
	$9 \times 5 \times 3$	2 L	$23 \times 13 \times 7$
Round Layer	$8 \times 1 1/2$	1.2 L	20×4
Cake Pan	$9 \times 1 1/2$	1.5 L	23×4
Pie Plate	$8 \times 1 1/4$	750 mL	20×3
	$9 \times 1 1/4$	1 L	23×3
Baking Dish	1 quart	1 L	—
or Casserole	$1 1/2$ quarts	1.5 L	—
	2 quarts	2 L	—